AMAZING ANIMALS

SEA SLUGS

BY ASHLEY GISH

CREATIVE EDUCATION • CREATIVE PAPERBACKS

Published by Creative Education
and Creative Paperbacks
P.O. Box 227, Mankato, Minnesota 56002
Creative Education and Creative Paperbacks
are imprints of The Creative Company
www.thecreativecompany.us

Design by The Design Lab
Production by Blue Design
Art direction by Wyeth Morgan

Images by Getty Images/A Mokhtari, 2, 3, 4, 6, 7, 8, 10, 11, 12, 13, 14, 15, 16, 18, 19, 20, 21, 22, 24, Antonio Camacho, 13, Giordano Cipriani, 14; Pexels/Thomas Bannenberg, cover, 1; Shutterstock/Ruslan Suseynov, 23; Unsplash/Ahmer Kalam, 10, Heidi Bruce, 6, 7, Jeff Talbott, 9, Pascal van de Vendel, 5, Swanson Chan, 18; Wikimedia Commons/Bernard DUPONT, 8, Diego Delso, 21, Izuzuki Diver, 11, Nhobgood, 2, rawpixel, 17, Taro Taylor, 16

Cataloging-in-Publication data is available from the Library of Congress.
Library Binding ISBN: 9798895810590
Paperback ISBN: 9798896800125
eBook ISBN: 9798895811856
LCCN: 2025011192

Printed in China

Table of Contents

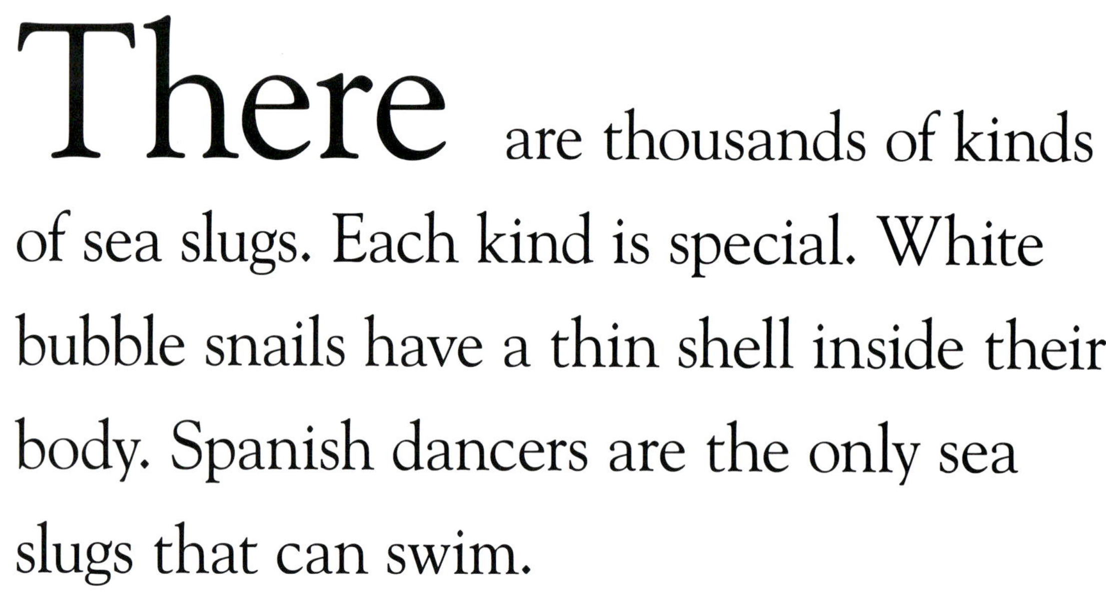

There are thousands of kinds of sea slugs. Each kind is special. White bubble snails have a thin shell inside their body. Spanish dancers are the only sea slugs that can swim.

Sea slugs are colorful. Hot pink, neon blue, and electric purple are common colors among sea slugs.

A sea slug's color depends on what it eats. Sea hares that eat red things are reddish-colored. Sea hares that eat green food are greenish.

Sea slugs are **mollusks**. This group of animals includes nudibranchs (NOO-di-branks), sea hares, and bubble snails. Sea slugs range in length from an eighth of an inch (3.1 millimeters) to 2.5 feet (76.2 centimeters).

mollusk a water-dwelling animal with a soft body

Most sea slugs have two club-shaped organs on top of their heads. These are used for smelling food and **predators**. Some sea slugs breathe through **gills** on their rear end. Others breathe using tube-shaped body parts on their back.

gill an organ that pulls oxygen from water instead of air

predator an animal that eats other animals

The sea bunny gets its name from its smelling organs and fluffy gills, which look like a bunny's ears and tail.

Sea slugs live in all the Earth's oceans. Many of the most colorful nudibranchs live in the Great Barrier Reef. Sea hares live in shallow water along rocky shorelines. Bubble snails live in tropical seagrass meadows.

Great Barrier Reef a coral reef system off Australia's northeast coast

Most sea slugs are poisonous. But they may still be eaten by some turtles, fish, and even other nudibranchs.

Sea slugs eat tiny sea animals, jellyfish, and plants. Blue dragon sea slugs steal toxins from the jellyfish they eat. The toxins stay inside the sea slug's skin. Most animals won't eat toxic sea slugs.

toxin poison that is harmful if eaten

Some sea slugs lay up to 500 eggs at a time.

Sea slugs gather in groups to find mates. Then, they lay eggs. All sea slugs can lay eggs. The eggs spiral out of the sea slug in a ribbon of **mucus** (MYOO-kus). There may be millions of eggs in the ribbon.

mucus slime made by the body

The mucus around the eggs is toxic to predators. It protects baby sea slugs growing inside the eggs. It may take up to 50 days for sea slugs to hatch. Some sea slugs live for up to six years.

Baby sea slugs look like tiny snails. Most kinds shed their shells after they hatch.

Sea slugs move slowly, at 0.2 miles (0.3 kilometers) per hour.

The emerald sea slug steals a special ability from algae. Algae gets energy from the sun. After the sea slug eats the algae, the slug can also get energy from the sun.

algae plant-like living things that grow in water

A bubble snail's thin shell is protected by the slug's body, which doesn't fit inside the shell.

Some sea slugs have a trick to get rid of **parasites**. If their body has too many parasites, the sea slug will split its body from its head. The head can grow a new body–heart, stomach, and all.

parasite an animal or plant that gets its food by living on or inside another animal or plant

A Sea Slug Tale

There are about 3,000 kinds of nudibranchs in the world. More than half of them live in the ocean around Japan. Many writers and artists in Japan have included nudibranchs in their work. These sea slugs can be found in animated movies, graphic novels, and shows.

Read More

Klepeis, Alicia Z. *Sea Slugs*. Minneapolis: Jump! 2020.

Murphy, Julie. Odd Bods: *The World's Unusual Animals*. Minneapolis: Millbrook Press, 2021.

Woodbury, Rebecca. *Mollusks*. Tempe, AZ: Real Science-4-Kids, 2022.

Websites

5 Species of Sea Slugs: A rainbow of life in our seas
https://www.mcsuk.org/news/sea-slugs-a-rainbow-of-life-in-our-seas
Learn about five amazing sea slugs.

Nudibranch
https://kids.nationalgeographic.com/animals/invertebrates/facts/nudibranch
Learn more about nudibranchs on National Geographic Kids' website.

This Jorunna sea slug looks like a tiny, fluffy "sea bunny"
https://thekidshouldseethis.com/post/this-jorunna-sea-slug-looks-like-a-tiny-fluffy-sea-bunny
Watch this video of the sea bunny in action.

Note: Every effort has been made to ensure that the websites listed above are suitable for children, that they have educational value, and that they contain no inappropriate material. However, because of the nature of the Internet, it is impossible to guarantee that these sites will remain active indefinitely or that their contents will not be altered.

Index